Gold Stars

This book belongs to:

Emily Rendall

I read the first story!

I read the second story!

I read the third story!

Level 2

Stories to Read

Written by Sue Graves
Illustrated by Alison Atkins, Jacqueline East
and Daniel Howarth

Language consultant: Betty Root

This is a Parragon book
This edition published in 2003

Parragon
Queen Street House
4 Queen Street
Bath, BA1 1HE, UK

ISBN 1-40542-812-0
Printed in China

Gold Stars

Stories to Read

Three Level 2 Stories

p

Contents

Notes for Parents

Reading with your child is an enjoyable and rewarding experience. **Gold Stars Stories to Read** encourage and support children who are learning to read.

There are four different reading levels within the **Stories to Read** series. Within each level, the books can be read in any order. The steps between the levels are deliberately small because it is so important, at this early stage, for children to succeed. Success creates confidence.

Starting to read

Start by reading the story aloud to your child, taking time to talk about the pictures. This will help your child to see that pictures often give clues about the story.

Over a period of time, try to read the same story several times so that your child becomes familiar with the story and the words and phrases. Gradually your child will want to read the story aloud with you. It helps to run your finger under the words as you say them.

Occasionally, stop and encourage your child to continue reading aloud without you. Join in again when your child needs help. This is the next step towards helping your child become an independent reader.

Finally, your child will be ready to read alone. Listen carefully to your child and give plenty of praise. Remember to make reading an enjoyable experience.

Using your Gold Stars stickers

You can use the **Gold Stars** stickers as a reward for effort as well as achievement. Learning to read is an exciting challenge for every child.

Remember these four important stages:

- Read the story **to** your child.
- Read the story **with** your child.
- Encourage your child to read **to you**.
- Listen to your child read **alone**.

Noisy Train

This is Noisy Train.
Noisy Train is very noisy.

He likes to blow his whistle.
"Toot, toot!"

He likes to blow it very loudly!

Every day Noisy Train saw Sheep.

"Toot, toot!" said Noisy Train. "Hello, Sheep!"

Every day Sheep got cross.

"Baa, baa!" said Sheep.
"What a noisy train!"

Every day Noisy Train saw Sheepdog.

“Toot, toot!” said Noisy Train. “Hello, Sheepdog!”

Every day Sheepdog got cross.

"Woof, woof!" said Sheepdog.
"What a noisy train!"

Sheep and Sheepdog went to see Noisy Train.

"You are too noisy," they said. "Stop blowing your whistle."

Noisy Train was sad.

"I'll stop blowing my whistle," he said.

The next day, Noisy Train saw Sheep.

But he didn't blow his whistle.

Sheep was pleased.

"Baa, baa!" she said.
"That's better."

Then Noisy Train saw Sheepdog.

But he didn't blow his whistle.

Sheepdog was pleased.

"Woof, woof!" he said.
"That's better."

But then Noisy Train saw the lambs.

The lambs were on the track.

"The lambs must be moved," said Noisy Train. "I must get Sheep and Sheepdog."

Noisy Train flashed his lights.
"Flash, flash!"

He puffed out steam.
"Puff, puff!"

But Sheep and Sheepdog did not come.

"I will have to blow my whistle," said Noisy Train. "Then Sheep and Sheepdog will come."

Noisy Train blew his whistle. "Toot, toot!" He blew it very loudly.

Sheep and Sheepdog came running. They got the lambs to move off the track.

“Baa, baa!” said Sheep. “Woof, woof!” said Sheepdog. “We’re glad you are a noisy train!”

Read these words. Look back in the story and find the words.

Noisy Train

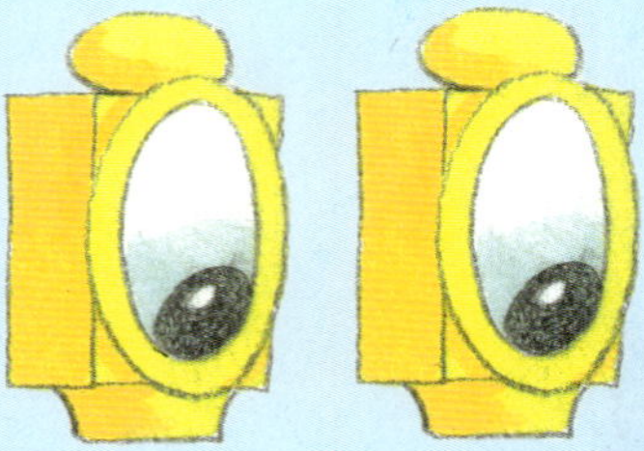

lights

Sheep

Sheepdog

lambs

track

Elephant's Birthday

It was Monday. Elephant was excited.

"It's my birthday," she said.
"I shall have a party."

Elephant went to find Monkey. "Puff, puff!" Monkey was busy blowing up balloons.

"Hello, Monkey!" said Elephant. "It's my birthday. Can you come to my party?"

"No, I can't," said Monkey. "I'm too busy blowing up this balloon."

“Oh dear!” said Elephant.
“Never mind. I’ll ask Lion.
Perhaps he can come.”

Elephant went to find Lion. "Flip, flap!" Lion was busy making a party hat.

"Hello, Lion!" said Elephant. "It's my birthday. Can you come to my party?"

"No, I can't," said Lion. "I'm too busy making this party hat."

"Oh dear!" said Elephant.
"Never mind. I'll ask Crocodile.
Perhaps she can come."

Elephant went to find Crocodile. "Pat, pat!" Crocodile was busy making a cake.

"Hello, Crocodile!" said Elephant. "It's my birthday. Can you come to my party?"

"No, I can't," said Crocodile. "I'm too busy making this cake."

"Oh dear!" said Elephant. "Everyone is too busy. Now I can't have a party!"

Elephant went off. She felt very sad. Just then, she met Giraffe.

“Why are you so sad?”
asked Giraffe.

“Everyone is too busy to come to my party,” said Elephant.

"Never mind!" said Giraffe. "Come with me. I have a surprise for you."

Giraffe took Elephant to the pool.

All the animals were at the pool.

"Surprise! Surprise!" they all shouted.

"Wow!" said Elephant.
"This is the best birthday party ever!"

Read these words. Look back in the story and find the words.

Elephant

cake

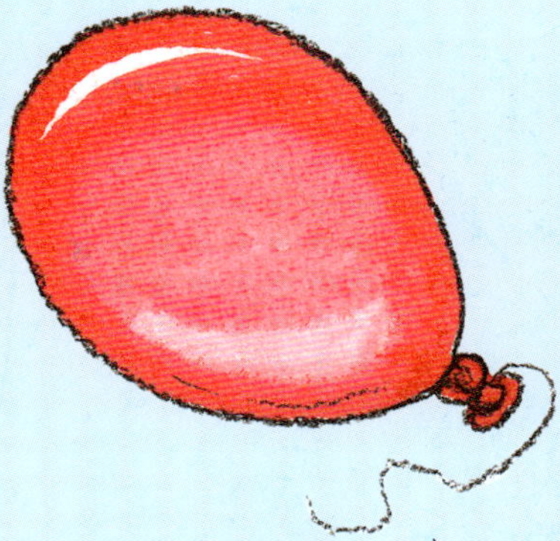

balloon

Giraffe

hat

Monkey

Sam Duckling Swims

This is Sam Duckling.
Sam lives by the pond.

He lives with Mummy Duck and the other ducklings.

"Jump in and swim," said Mummy Duck one day.

The ducklings jumped in the pond.

Splash! They swam and swam.

But Sam didn't jump in.

"Jump in and swim," said Mummy Duck. "It's fun!"

Sam looked into the water.

"The water is too deep," he said. "I'll stay here."

"Jump in and swim," said Mummy Duck. "It's fun!"

Sam put his wing in the water.

"The water is too cold," said Sam. "I'll stay here."

"Quack, quack!" said the ducklings. "Swim with us, Mummy! Swim with us!"

Mummy Duck went off with the ducklings. Sam began to cry.

Just then Frog popped up.
He popped up out of the water.

"Hello, Sam," said Frog.
"Come and swim. It's fun!"

"I don't want to," said Sam. "The water is too deep and too cold."

Frog sat by Sam.

“I’ll help you swim,” he said.

Frog got a lily-pad.

"Sit on the lily-pad, Sam," he said.

Sam sat on the lily-pad.

Frog pulled Sam along.

"Now splash your feet,"
said Frog.

Sam splashed his feet.

"Quack, quack!" said Sam.
"This is fun!"

"Now get off the lily-pad," said Frog.

Sam got off the lily-pad.

"I'm swimming!" said Sam.

“Quack, quack!” said Mummy Duck. “Well done, Sam!”

Read these words. Look back in the story and find the words.

Sam

Mummy Duck

pond

ducklings

Frog

lily-pad

Gold Stars

Level 2 stories are for children who are beginning to read.

- Familiar, repeated vocabulary
- Short sentences
- Large, clear type
- Pictures that support the text
- Review activity

Gold Stars

Gold Stars Stories to Read
encourage and support
children who are learning to read.

- **Level 1:** for children who are ready to begin learning to read.
- **Level 2:** for children who can recognize simple words and phrases.
- **Level 3:** for beginner readers who can read short sentences with help.
- **Level 4:** for more confident readers who are beginning to read alone.